T0072246

Alexei's week

by Antonia Barber

NATIONAL GEOGRAPHIC LEARNING | CENGAGE

It's Sunday at 3:00 a.m. Alexei can't sleep! He is worried about going to his new school.

It's Monday at 7:15 a.m. The bus is late.

Mr. Clark is the bus driver.

It's 10:00 a.m. Alexei is lost.
Where is his homeroom?

It's Tuesday at 12:00 p.m. Alexei eats lunch.

Alexei sits by himself.

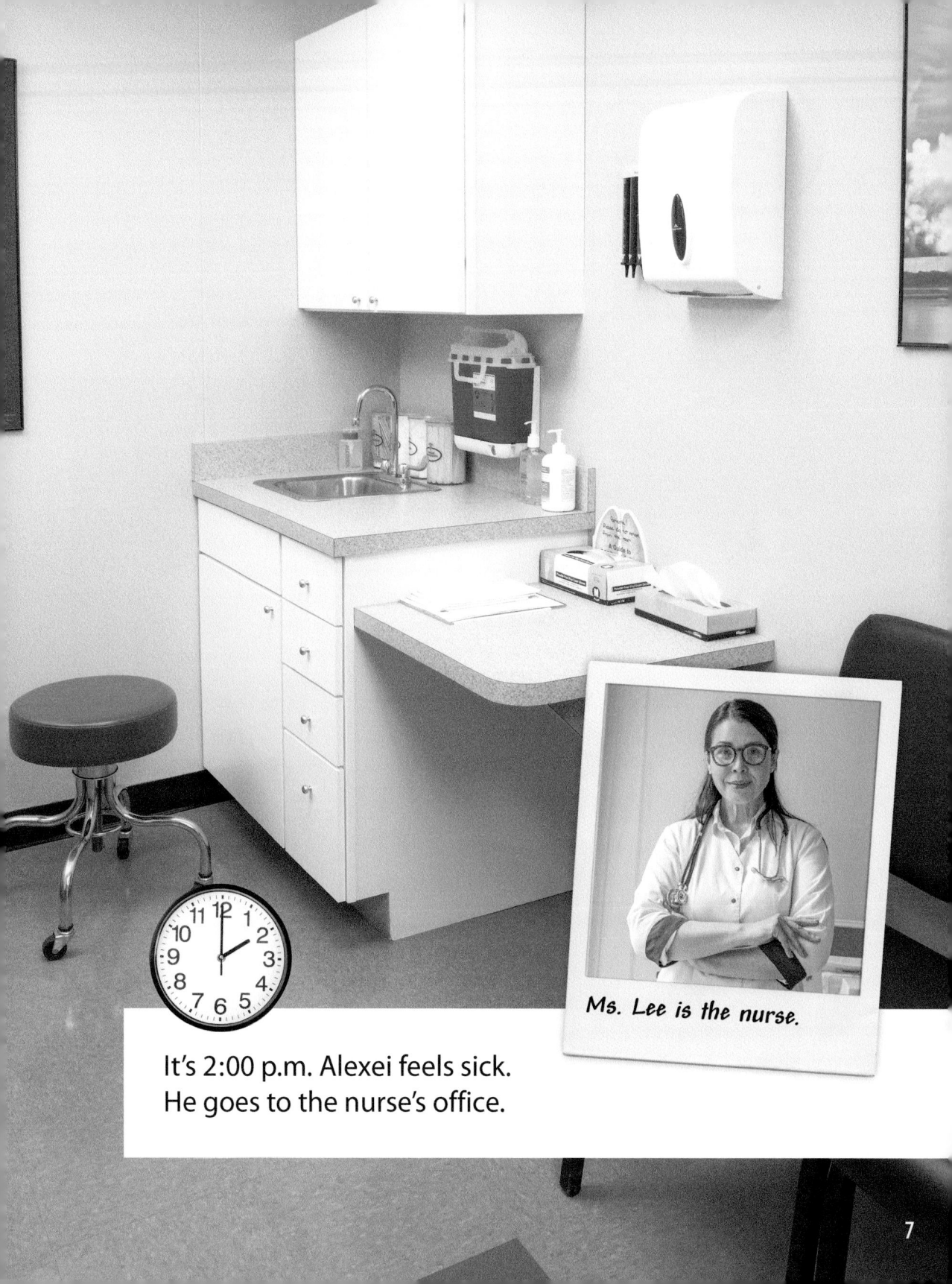

It's 2:00 p.m. Alexei feels sick.
He goes to the nurse's office.

It's Wednesday at 8:15 a.m. Alexei is late for school. He goes to the principal's office.

It's 1:30 p.m. Alexei needs a lab partner.

It's Thursday at 12:00 p.m. Alexei drops his lunch tray.

Hugo helps Alexei pick up his tray.

Hugo's mom drives Alexei home.

It's 3:00 p.m.
Alexei misses the bus.

It's Friday. Alexei has a good day.

SATURDAY
6
13
20
He finds his classroom.
He eats lunch with friends.
He sits with Yana on the bus.

It's Saturday at 11:00 a.m. Alexei helps his dad in the yard.

Alexei cuts the grass.

It's 2:00 p.m. Alexei goes to a movie with Hugo.

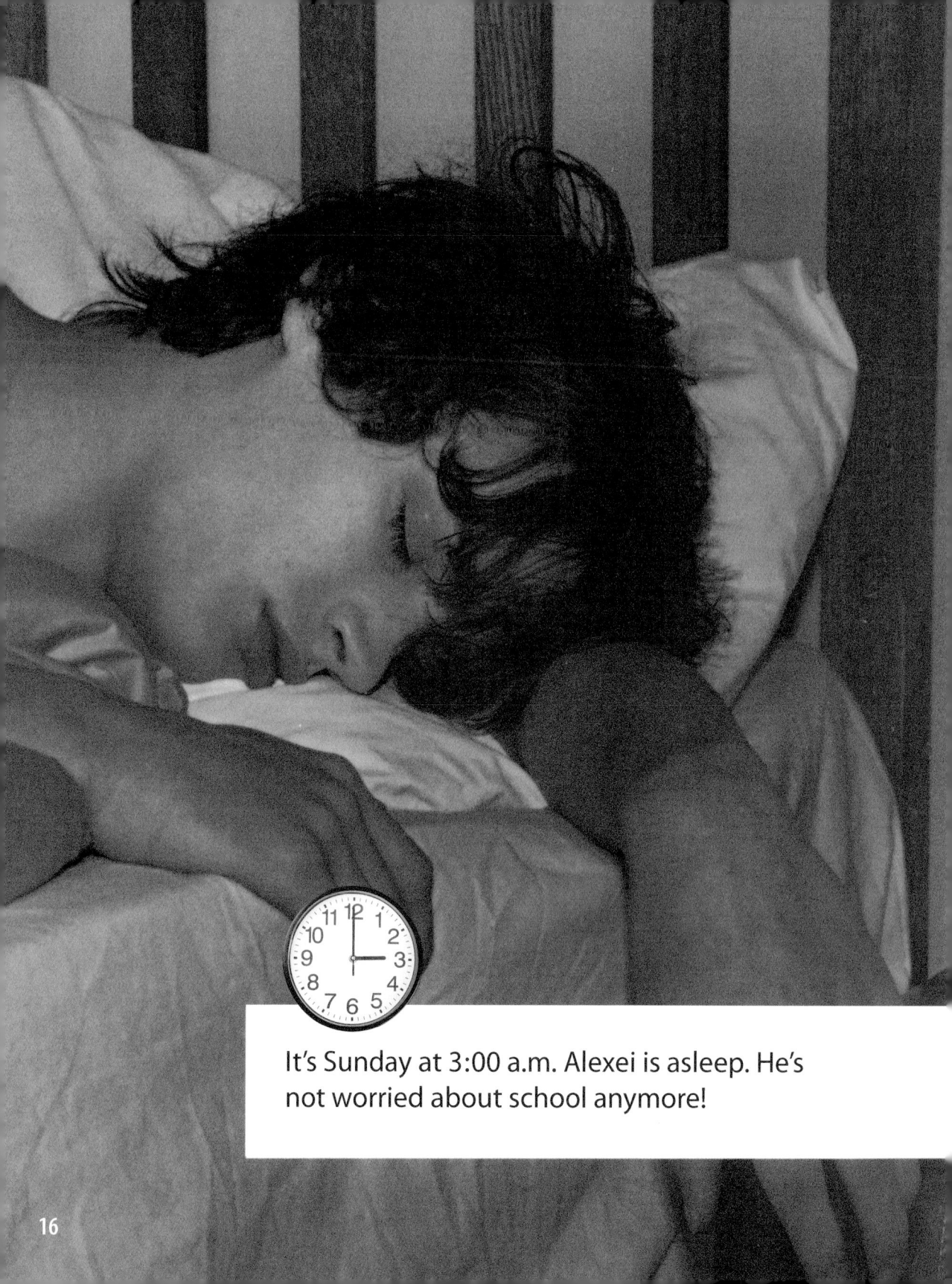

It's Sunday at 3:00 a.m. Alexei is asleep. He's not worried about school anymore!